A story by
Roy Etherton
Illustrated by Leon Baxter

LION PUBLISHING

Lion Publishing
121 High Street, Berkhamsted, Herts, England

First edition 1976

ISBN 0 85648 040 1

Printed in Britain by
Purnell and Sons Ltd, Paulton

It was pouring with rain.

Sarah, Tim and John stared gloomily out of the window. They couldn't go out, and there was nothing to do. They were bored and cross. Would the rain never stop?

'What long faces,' said a voice behind them – and there was Grandma. The children cheered up at once. Perhaps she would tell them a story. They all loved Grandma's stories.

'That's better,' Grandma said. 'I don't like to see grey faces as well as a grey day!' She looked thoughtful.'Though some people are like that all the time. The world is always grey for them, whether it's sunny or raining.'

'What do you mean?' said Sarah.

'Sit down by me,' said Grandma. 'And I'll tell you a story . . .

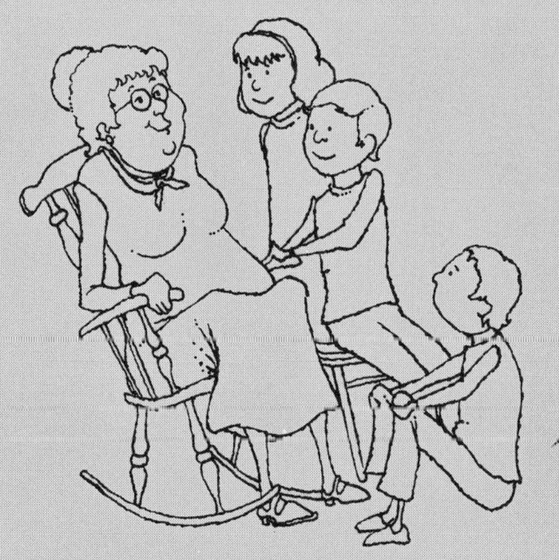

There was once a land called Greyland, where everything was grey.

The sky was grey. The grass was grey. The flowers were grey. Every day it looked like rain.

Even the people were grey.

Every morning they pulled back their curtains on another grey day. They put on their grey clothes and ran downstairs to a grey breakfast. Then they shut their grey front doors and hurried past the grey shops to catch the grey bus to work. Grey spotted dogs barked as they passed. The children played with their grey toys, and went to school in grey school clothes.

It was very dull.

There was no colour anywhere.

No cheerful red. No orange. No blue.
No green. No yellow. Not even brown!

But the people didn't mind
– because they didn't know.
They had never seen a blue sky,
or green grass, or yellow buttercups.
So they were happy enough in
Greyland, in a grey sort of way.

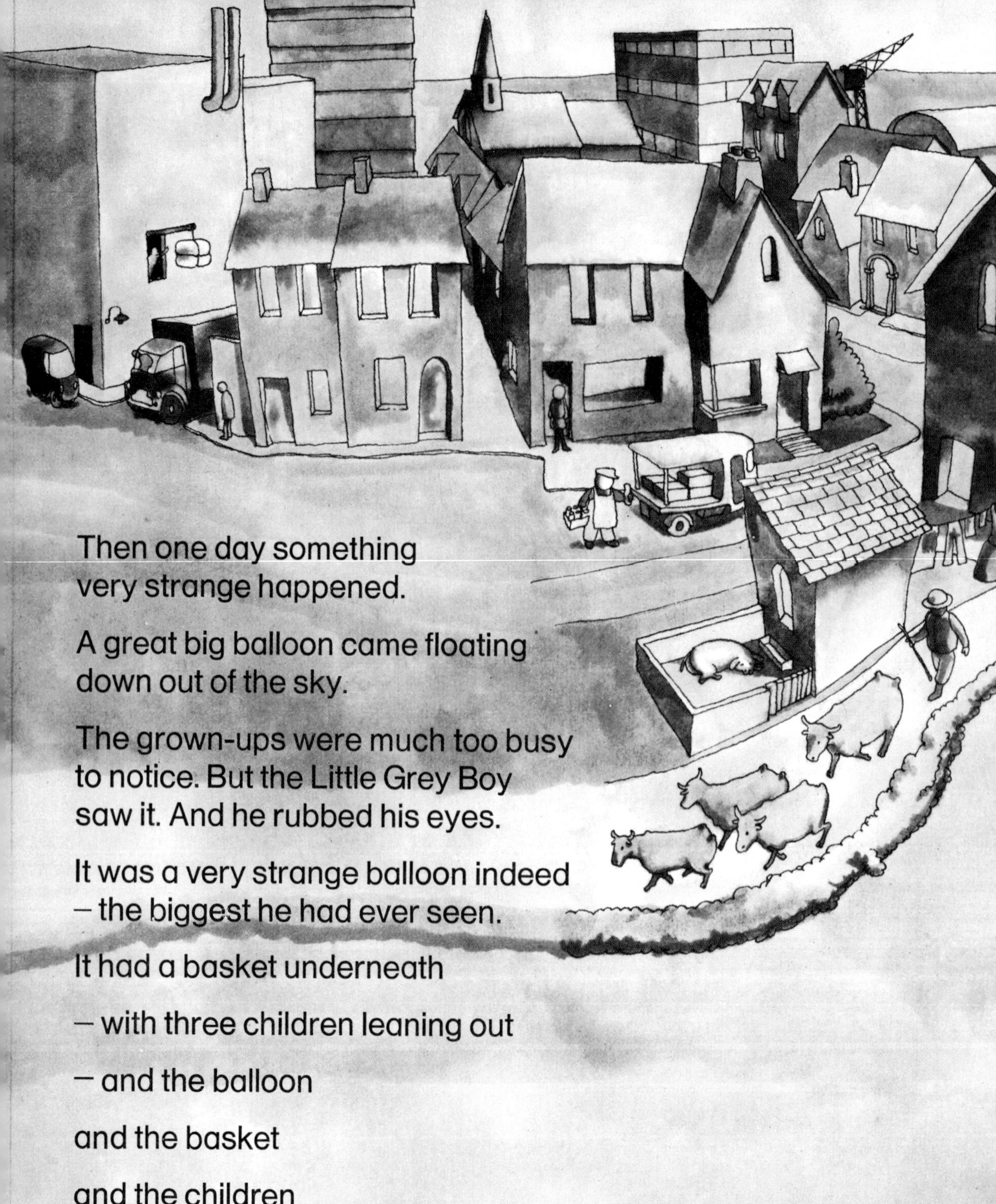

Then one day something very strange happened.

A great big balloon came floating down out of the sky.

The grown-ups were much too busy to notice. But the Little Grey Boy saw it. And he rubbed his eyes.

It was a very strange balloon indeed – the biggest he had ever seen.

It had a basket underneath

– with three children leaning out

– and the balloon

and the basket

and the children

weren't grey!

The balloon was coming to land.

The Little Grey Boy ran to meet it.

The basket bumped gently on the grey grass, and Sarah, Tim and John climbed out.

The Little Grey Boy stared and stared. He just couldn't help it.

He stared at their brown hair and their rosy cheeks.

He stared at Sarah's bright blue dress.

He stared at Tim's red trousers and his yellow jersey.

He stared at John's brown jeans and his green striped shirt.

He'd never seen anything like it before.

The children stared back at the Little Grey Boy. How strange he looked. Where could they be?

They looked at the sky, and that was grey.

They looked at the grass, and that was grey.

They looked at the flowers, and they were grey.

There were no colours at all. They had never seen anything like it before.

'Where are we?' they asked the Little Grey Boy. 'Why is everything grey? Where have all the colours gone?'

'This is Greyland,' said the Little Grey Boy. 'What are colours? And where did you get your lovely clothes?'

'Colours are – blue,' said Sarah, 'like my dress.'

'And red,' said Tim, 'like my trousers – and yellow like my jersey.'

'And green, like the stripes on my shirt,' said John. 'And brown, like my jeans.'

'Oooh!' breathed the Little Grey Boy. 'So that's what colours are. I like colours. I like them very much. I'd like to wear blue trousers and a bright red jersey!'

'It's not just clothes,' said Tim.
'We come from a land of colour.

The sky is blue,

the grass is green,

poppies are red,

and buttercups are yellow.

Everything has its own colour.
It's lovely.'

'A Land of Colour,' sighed the Little Grey Boy. He'd been quite happy with grey before. Now it made him feel sad. If only someone could make his Greyland into a Land of Colour.

Then he had an idea.

'Come with me,' said the Little Grey Boy. 'We'll go and see the Mayor. He'll tell us what to do.'

When they came to the town, how everyone stared! They rubbed their eyes.

'Where are you going?' they cried to the Little Grey Boy.

'We're going to see the Mayor,' said the Little Grey Boy. 'We want him to make our Greyland into a Land of Colour.'

'Colour?' said the people, staring at the children.

'Colour?' they said, looking at Sarah's blue dress, and Tim's red trousers, and John's striped shirt. 'What a good idea. We'll come with you.'

And they all stopped what they were doing, and went along too.

Rat-a-tat-tat!

The Little Grey Boy knocked at the Mayor's front door.

'Please, Mr Mayor,' said the Little Grey Boy, 'we want to make our Greyland into a Land of Colour. Can you tell us how?'

'Colour?' said the Mayor, staring at the children.

'Colour?' he said, looking at Sarah's blue dress, and Tim's red trousers, and John's striped shirt. 'What a good idea! We'll go and ask the Wizard who lives in The Hole.'

So off they went.

When they came to The Hole, it had no front door – so the Mayor called down.

'Wizard,' he said, 'please come up and help us. We want to make our Greyland into a Land of Colour. Can you tell us how?'

The Wizard popped his head up out of The Hole.

'Colour?' said the Wizard, staring at the children.

'Colour?' he said, looking at Sarah's blue dress, and Tim's red trousers, and John's striped shirt.
'What a good idea! I'll just look through my book of spells.'
And he turned the pages of his big grey book till he found the place.

'I'm going to make it snow,' he said. 'And when the snow melts, there'll be colour everywhere. Just you watch.'

So the Wizard made his spell, and it began to snow.

It snowed and it snowed till everything was covered.

Then the sun came out and the snow began to melt.

And everything was

ORANGE!

'Oh dear!' said the Mayor and the children and the people. 'That's no good. It's worse than it was before. Please change it all back.
We'll go and see the Witch of the Talking Forest.'

So the Wizard unmade his spell,
and off they went.

The trees swayed and whispered as they passed, rustling their thin grey leaves.

In the middle of the Talking Forest, they found the Witch. She was stroking her big grey cat.

'Witch,' said the Mayor, 'please help us. We want to make our Greyland into a Land of Colour. Can you tell us how?'

'Colour?' said the Witch, staring at the children.

'Colour?' she said, looking at Sarah's blue dress, and Tim's red trousers, and John's striped shirt. 'What a good idea! You shall have some of my magic paint that never runs out.'

So she gave them each a tin of her magic paint, and a brush to paint with.

'Paint everything the colour you want,' she said. 'I shall paint the sky.' And she climbed up onto her broomstick.

So everyone set to work.

They painted the grass and they painted the insects.

They painted the trees and they painted the leaves.

They painted the fruit and they painted the flowers.

They even painted themselves!

But it wasn't any use.

It all looked wrong.

The ladybirds were purple and the beetles were pink.

The trees had blue and white spots.

The grass was yellow and the flowers were striped.

And the Witch had painted the sky a nasty shade of green! It was dreadful.

'Oh dear!' said the Mayor and the children and the people. 'That's no good. It's worse than it was before.' And they all set to work to wash the paint off.

Then the Little Grey Boy said to the children:

'The Mayor can't do it.
And the Wizard can't do it.
And the Witch can't do it.
How can we make our Greyland into a Land of Colour?'

Sarah thought, and then she said, 'Why don't you ask the Maker?'

There was a long pause.
The people hung their heads.
Why, they had forgotten all about the Maker.

Now they began to remember.
They remembered stories of long ago – stories of The Beginning, of a beautiful Land of Colour, where the Maker and his people were happy together. Before things went wrong and the colours faded away.

Yes, they would ask the Maker.
And that was what they did. They said they were sorry for forgetting him.
And they asked him to make their Greyland into a Land of Colour – please!

Then they waited.

They waited all day – and nothing happened.

But the very next morning there was a most tremendous thunderstorm.

The sky grew darker and darker. Great drops of rain began to fall. And in next to no time it was simply pouring.

But there was something different about the rain.

The Little Grey Boy was the first to notice.

IT WAS RAINING IN COLOURS!

Every colour you can think of
– and every colour in the right place!

The green drops fell on the leaves and the grass.
The brown drops fell on the earth.
Red drops fell on the poppies, and yellow drops fell on the buttercups.

When the people saw it they shouted for joy – and they all ran out to catch the sparkling raindrops.

Then a lovely thing happened. They weren't grey people any more! The raindrops fell on their hair and turned it brown. Their cheeks grew rosy. And as for their clothes – you've never seen such colours. Everyone had the colours he liked best.

The Little Grey Boy was a Brown Boy now. He danced and sang – in his new blue trousers and his bright red jersey. He had never been so happy.

Then the rain stopped and the sun came out – a golden sun in the clear blue sky.

It shone on the happy, laughing people.

The stream in the meadow looked blue as the sky.

Robin redbreast sang from his branch.

Butterflies settled on the gleaming flowers.

And every drop of rain sparkled in the light.

The people thanked the Maker. 'Thank you,' they said, 'for our Land of Colour. We promise we'll never forget you again.'

'Goodbye,' said Sarah to the Little Grey Boy who was a Brown Boy now.

'Goodbye Land of Colour,' said Tim and John.

Then they climbed back into the basket of the great balloon – and a little breeze caught them gently, up and away.